LifeCaps Presents:

Blacklisted

A Biography of Dalton Trumbo

By Jennifer Warner

BookCaps™ Study Guides

www.bookcaps.com

© 2014. All Rights Reserved.

Cover Image © mumindurmaz35 - Fotolia.com

Table of Contents

About LifeCaps

LifeCaps is an imprint of BookCaps™ Study Guides. With each book, a lesser known or sometimes forgotten life is recapped. We publish a wide array of topics (from baseball and music to literature and philosophy), so check our growing catalogue regularly (**www.bookcaps.com**) to see our newest books.

Introduction

Dalton Trumbo was the highest paid screenwriter in Hollywood when he was investigated as a Communist during America's Red Scare of the 1940s. He was ultimately sent to jail and placed on an industry blacklist that would make him unhirable. His exile lasted 13 years during which time he was forced to write screenplays under assumed names. While on the Hollywood blacklist Trumbo's writing won two Academy Awards, Oscars the public would never know about.

Chapter 1: Early Life

A sense of place would come to be a recurring theme in the works of Dalton Trumbo and his first place was in the Colorado mining town of Montrose. Nestled into the San Juan Mountains in the southwestern portion of the Centennial State, Montrose was scarcely a generation old when James Dalton Trumbo entered the world on December 9, 1905.

The Trumbos were an old Virginian family established by Hans Jacob Trumbo in 1736. Hans was born in Alsace-Lorraine in 1709 at the crossroads of France, Germany, Switzerland and Belgium. After sailing to America, he passed on the more developed regions of the Virginia Tidewater, and instead settled in the wilderness of Rockingham County in the Shenandoah Mountains. Hans Jacob would father eight children with Mary Dorothea Trumbo and live long enough to see the United States become an independent country and his fellow Virginian, George Washington, take the office of President.

Subsequent generations of Trumbos would migrate to become some of the first settlers in the new states of Kentucky and Ohio. Trumbo men would fight in the American Revolution, the Indian Wars, and for both the Confederacy and the Union in the Civil War. By the time Orus Bonham Trumbo was born on June 14, 1876 in Albion, Ohio he was in the fourth generation of the family to live in the Buckeye State.

Like his ancestors, Orus Trumbo drifted westward. In Colorado, he made the acquaintance of Maud Tillery, whose Missouri-born parents had built one of the first houses in Montrose County. Millard Fillmore Tillery, named for the recently departed President from the Whig Party, was a rough and tumble frontier cattleman and rancher. When Orus began courting the eldest of his five children, Millard Tillery was serving one of his two terms as a no-nonsense sheriff of Montrose County where the lawman had a reputation for always getting his man.

Orus Trumbo tried various occupations in Colorado but nothing seemed to stick. He was a farmer and a teacher and operated a small commercial apiary. In 1908, Orus and Maud packed up their only child and moved sixty miles north to Grand Junction. Although boasting a population of only 5,000, Grand Junction, named for the confluence of the Gunnison and Colorado Rivers, was the "big city" in western Colorado. Orus Trumbo found a job as a shoe store clerk, selling footwear to the farmers who grew most of the state's fruit in the high desert flatlands.

While young Dalton exhibited a mischievous streak in elementary school that would several times single him out for reprimands, the Trumbo family grew to include daughters Catherine and Elizabeth. The only Trumbo boy would spend the rest of his childhood in Grand Junction until leaving for the University of Colorado. While most boys of the early 20th century frontier pursued what Theodore Roosevelt called "the strenuous life" of sports and the outdoors, Dalton Trumbo channeled the energies of youth elsewhere. Although poor, his parents always managed to keep the house filled with books and magazines which Dalton devoured.

While in school, Trumbo landed a part-time job as a cub reporter for the *Grand Junction Sentinel*. He was soon devoting so much time to his scoops around town that he was bringing more money back in to the house than his father. The only thing that distracted Dalton from pursuing his journalism assignments was performing on the debating team in school.

When he was 18 years old, Trumbo traveled east to Boulder to matriculate at the University of Colorado. He quickly began working on *The Silver and Gold*, the university student newspaper, and helping out on the yearbook. Trumbo also contributed pieces to the school humor magazine. Before the school year was out he had landed a job on the *Boulder Daily Camera* that had been dishing out news on Colorado's Front Range since 1890.

Trumbo's collegiate career was off to a grand start, but during his freshman year, Orus Trumbo was let go at the shoe store and the family moved out to Los Angeles when his health started failing. With no money to pay for further schooling and his family ailing, Trumbo closed out his schooling in Boulder and reluctantly moved to California.

In Trumbo's mind, he would enroll in the University of Southern California and pick up his writing career as he had in Colorado. But when he arrived in 1925 he found the Trumbo family in dire straits. His father was too ill to work, and it would turn out he had contracted pernicious anemia, although no one knew it since Orus and Maud had joined Mary Baker Eddy's Church of Christ, Scientist, which frowned on medical intervention. The disease would kill Orus Trumbo before the year was out.

To bring money into the household for his widowed mother and two young sisters, Trumbo took a job with the Davis Perfection Bakery, the city's largest. He only saw wrapping fresh bread as stop-gap employment but would stay at the bakery for more than eight years, for the remainder of the Roaring Twenties and into the first years of the Great Depression. He managed to attend some classes at the University of Southern California, but it would be the Davis Perfection Bakery that would be the real breeding ground for many of the themes and ideas that would inhabit Dalton's Trumbo's writing.

Chapter 2: Early Career

One thing Trumbo saw every day at the bakery was the stark situational differences between the bosses and the workers. He had witnessed what he considered the unfair conditions under which his father toiled for years and he was now experiencing the same realities. In the world of "us" versus "them" Trumbo was fully on the side of the worker, and viewed authority with healthy contempt - an attitude that would come to define his career and his life in later years.

Trumbo would visit the chasm between the powerful and powerless in many screenplays, but while he sided with the little guy he was never romantic about his struggles. Rather, he saw poverty as something to be avoided at all costs, and he would work feverishly to insure that it would not be his fate. "I never considered the working class anything other than something to get out of," he said.

Trumbo's sometimes indifferent regard to the law began to take shape in his time on the bakery floor as well. Prohibition was in effect during his stint at Davis Perfection Bakery, and it was routine for police to stop in and pick up breads and cakes, compliments of the management. In return, the cops would leave behind a bottle of whiskey from time to time. Trumbo had no qualms about selling illegal booze himself. He would stop into a speakeasy for a drink and after sampling it slam the glass on the table and proclaim to anyone within earshot that he had been served lousy liquor. He would then produce his own bottle of mash and pass out samples, assisted by a hydrometer for everyone to see the competing alcohol contents.

Trumbo's career as a bootlegger was short-lived, however. Not from any attacks of law abiding righteousness, but because two competitors were gunned down in his neighborhood. After shuttering the liquor distribution business, he made a little money on the side repossessing motorcycles.

During his stay at the bakery, Trumbo, by his reckoning, churned out six novel-length manuscripts and 88 short stories. All were rejected. He also wrote movie reviews for local trade publications as the first "talkies" were being introduced into theaters. In 1932, he sold his first article - a piece based on his bootlegging experiences - to *Vanity Fair* magazine that led managing editor Clare Boothe Brokaw, to hire him as a Hollywood correspondent. When Brokaw would come to appear in headlines in coming years as America's first woman appointed to a major overseas ambassadorial post it would be as Clare Boothe Luce, after she married the founder of *TIME* magazine, Henry Luce.

Trumbo wrote spare, pointed prose and he wrote fast. As a freelancer in the depths of the Great Depression he sold short stories, and a luncheon interview with Austrian actor Baron Frederick de Reichenberg about Hollywood's mistakes depicting Europe on celluloid led to Trumbo ghostwriting his autobiography, Prince Metternich in Love and War. The extra publicity did no favors for the European nobleman, who was arrested in 1935 for overstaying his entry permit that expired in 1932.

One of Trumbo's most regular assignments was as a writer and critic at *The Hollywood Spectator*. When the magazine offered him the position of managing editor, the 27-year old Trumbo, who had spent nearly every day of his California life in the bakery since coming to Los Angeles eight years earlier, was able to quit and focus his career on writing. But the magazine was never able to cover its bills, and Trumbo would never receive his full salary.

Trumbo saw himself as a novelist, but when an opportunity to become a reader on the lot of Warner Brothers Studios in the story department came along in 1934, he jumped at it. The steady paychecks freed him to work on a novel that was set in the small fictional western town of Shale City, which bore a striking resemblance to Grand Junction. Its title, *Eclipse*, was a tip-off that Trumbo did not wax nostalgic for his old hometown.

His main character, John Abbott, was a self-made businessman who fought against the backward and introverted beliefs of his surroundings. Abbott ended up owning the largest department store in Shale City, and was the town's most vociferous booster and benefactor. Back in Grand Junction, the most influential business man was William J. Moyer, who owned the Fair Department Store on Main Street that was the biggest in western Colorado. Moyer gave money to build mountain roads into the isolated region, and donated $25,000 to build the community's first public swimming pool.

In Trumbo's novel, Abbott becomes Shale City's leading philanthropist, giving away money for public causes and private citizens. However, after the stock market crashes he dies poor and alone, his good deeds forgotten. Moyer, 70 years old at the time of the Wall Street implosion in 1929, was also financially ruined. It would not take much imagination for readers of *Eclipse* to connect Abbott to Moyer and Shale City to Grand Junction.

Eclipse was bought by an English publisher, and although the book never received widespread distribution in America, some copies made their way to Grand Junction. The public library would report that it could never keep the novel on its shelves since copies would be checked out and never returned. For years afterward there would be stories, most likely apocryphal, that townsfolk would burn copies of *Eclipse* and hurl them into the Colorado River. Nonetheless his debut novel boosted Trumbo's name in the writing community, and he was able to sell a story to the *Saturday Evening Post*, the country's most popular magazine.

As his twenties were coming to a close in the fall of 1935, Trumbo signed a seven-year contract with Warner Brothers to be in a junior writer. He was still looking at the movies as a necessary evil rather than a career ambition. He inserted in the contract the right to produce three more novels for his British publisher. He also included a list of 41 short story titles and two novels that he had already written to which he would retain rights. In fact, he had written none of those, but he wanted to make sure that his future best work could be shoveled toward a book publisher and not the movies if need be. Trumbo was applying the lessons learned from the bakery already: never trust your bosses, and never be overly burdened by the propriety of the law.

Those guiding principles showed up in Trumbo's work for the movies right from the beginning. His first screenplay was for a B-movie called Road Gang that came with the tagline: They're Fugitives From a ROAD GANG ... and They'll Never Go Back Alive! The fugitive in question is a newspaperman who is wrongly thrown in prison by more powerful men after writing a scathing revelatory article on political corruption. The hero stays true to his beliefs as he skirts the rules before becoming exonerated.

His career at Warner Brothers would soon follow an analogous course as his first movie. Trumbo signed on with the Screen Writers Guild, a labor union headed by writer John Howard Lawson that agitated for screenwriters to receive the same copyright protection on their material that writers in other were media were afforded. After Lawson traveled to Washington to testify in front of the House of Representatives' Patent Committee in 1936, less rabble-rousing members of the union broke away to form the more conservative Screen Playwrights.

Studio moguls naturally favored the Screen Playwrights. Jack Warner, even though he green-lit many films that portrayed President Franklin Roosevelt's New Deal in a favorable light, nonetheless decreed that his writers become members of the Screen Playwrights. Trumbo refused and, after only two films and less than a year, his contract was voided. He became even more active in the Screen Writers' Guild by editing its official publication, The Screen Writer.

Trumbo was blacklisted but not out of work long. Within a few weeks he signed on with Columbia Pictures, headed by Harry Cohn. Cohn was a working class kid from New York City who began his rise to Hollywood moguldom as a streetcar conductor. Columbia had only recently shaken its image as a B-movie studio with the smash success of the Clark Gable and Claudette Colbert collaboration in *It Happened One Night*. Cohn did not build a stable of stars like other studios but hired talent as budgets would allow.

Cohn reveled in his reputation as the most tyrannical of Hollywood bosses. Even as he took control of Columbia Pictures he remained the production chief. A favorite ploy was to summon new writers to his palatial offices after a few weeks on the job and theatrically tear up their latest work in front of the scribes. If Cohn was greeted by groveling in response the writer was dismissed. If there was objection the job was saved, especially if the writer could prove that the autocratic studio boss had never read the script.

Trumbo weathered Cohn's initiation tests and was put to work producing a Depression-era escapist romp called *Tugboat Princess*, about a small girl who is adopted by a crusty old sea captain after her parents are drowned at sea. He followed up by working on The Devil's Playground with Dolores del Rio, the first Mexican actress to achieve Hollywood stardom, in the lead female role. Both were formulaic pictures produced according to Cohn's exacting direction.

None of these minor projects was swaying Trumbo from his ambition to be a serious writer of novels. He became even more certain his future lay elsewhere on a spring evening in 1936 when Earl Felton, a fellow screenwriter, said to him, "I know the girl you should marry." The two drove in Trumbo's Packard roadster to a Hollywood drive-in, where a 19-year old refugee from Fresno named Cleo Fincher was a car-hop with a talent for juggling water glasses for tips. Trumbo proposed marriage on the spot.

Fincher laughed off the proposal since she was already engaged, but Trumbo's impulsive craziness left its mark. Fincher's intended forced her into a hasty marriage and Trumbo, filled with equal parts suspicion and desperation, hired a private detective to investigate the newly- betrothed husband. It turned out he was already married. The union was quickly annulled and the besotted screenwriter was back in the picture.

Trumbo became a regular at the drive-in, always leaving enormous tips. Cleo saved the gratuities and after a year returned the money to him; she would require courting, not purchasing. Cleo Fincher was everything Dalton Trumbo was not. She was vivacious and athletic and loved a good time while he would spend most days hunched over a typewriter or immersed in a book. Nonetheless, the two were married on March 13, 1938.

Trumbo had put his pursuit of Fincher above all else in his life. He left Columbia Pictures and put in a lackluster stint at Metro-Goldwyn-Mayer. Now that he and Cleo were married he tossed aside Hollywood pretensions altogether, and the young marrieds moved to a run-down 320-acre ranch in Ventura County, two hours away from any movie studio. Trumbo was prepared to channel his Colorado youth, fix up the Lazy-T, and hunker down to become a writer of serious, substantial works.

The ranch was coddled in the mountains of the Los Padres National Forest, about 60 miles due north of Los Angeles. The closest neighbor was five miles down the road. In time there would be cows, horses, pigs and chickens. Peacocks would strut the grounds and there would be a pet goat named Ingrid. There was a lake on the ranch, and it got cold enough in the high desert in the winter for Dalton to see snow, like he had in Colorado.

The Trumbos also started a family on the ranch. Their first child Nikola was born in January of 1939 and his brother Christopher followed a year later. The family was completed in 1945 with the arrival of Melissa, who was always known as Mitzi. Meanwhile, Trumbo began work on a novel based on an article he had read about a Canadian army officer who returned from World War I severely disfigured, and was visited by the Prince of Wales.

Johnny Got His Gun turned out to be the type of work that is included in the first line of an author's obituary. The anti-war novel follows the plight of Joe Bonham who returns from World War I after an artillery shell blast on the last day of the war claims both his arms, both his legs and all of his face, leaving him only with his life and his mind. After vainly trying to suffocate himself, Joe wants to be displayed as a symbol of the horrors of war. After he realizes that he will neither be allowed to die nor protest war, he must fight to retain his sanity by reminiscing about his former life and reflecting on the realities of war. Written as threats of war swirled across Europe and released two days after Germany invaded Poland to start World War II, *Johnny Got His Gun* won a National Book Award as the Most Original Book of 1939.

Even as Trumbo was removing himself from Hollywood, his star was ascending in the movie capital. While he scarcely hid his disdain for the film business, his work on the backlots had imbued Trumbo with a writing style made for movies. In 1938, Trumbo was hired by RKO Pictures, known primarily as the studio where Fred Astaire and Ginger Rogers made musicals, to work on their B-movie unit.

At RKO, Trumbo began by returning to a familiar theme: the struggle between the powerful and the powerless, although played with a light touch. In *Fugitives for a Night*, Matt Ryan is a Hollywood go-fer whose entire existence is at the whims of his bosses, to the point that he takes the rap for one of their murders before being exonerated in the end. The success of *Fugitives for a Night* begat *A Man to Remember* crafted around another of Trumbo's favorite themes: the honor of holding to one's beliefs. It, too, became a moneymaker and Trumbo settled in as one of Hollywood's busiest and highest paid screenwriters with six film credits in both 1939 and 1940.

In 1940, RKO had a property called *Kitty Foyle* about a plucky shopgirl based on a bestselling 1939 novel by Christopher Morley. Studio star Ginger Rogers was cast in the lead and Donald Ogden Stewart, who had won an Academy Award for *The Philadelphia Story* earlier that year, had written a screenplay adaption. But RKO executives considered Stewart's script "unshootable" and approached Trumbo. He agreed to rework the script on one condition: the studio tear up his contract. RKO agreed.

Trumbo's gamble on his talent was well-founded. *Kitty Foyle* went on to be nominated for an Oscar for Best Picture and Trumbo received his first nomination for Best Screenwriter. Neither won, but Rogers came home in 1941 with an Academy Award for Best Actress. Now a free agent, Trumbo was more in demand than ever.

With the coming of World War II, Dalton Trumbo went to work with the United States Army Air Forces in the Pacific Theater. He visited injured troops in military hospitals and helped the Navy on a film project that was eventually canceled. His war experiences informed his writing during this time.

Trumbo wrote the screenplay for A Guy Named Joe with Spencer Tracy and Irene Dunne about a World War II fighter pilot who is killed and goes to heaven before being sent back to earth as a guardian angel for other pilots. In later years Stephen Spielberg would cite A Guy Named Joe as a major influence on his movie-making. Another wartime script was Trumbo's adaptation of the daring mission of Colonel Jimmy Doolittle, a one-time air racer, to carry out a raid on Japan in *Thirty Seconds over Tokyo*. His screenplay for *Tender Comrade* is one of the few depictions of a war bride ever put to film. During the war Trumbo also penned *Our Vines Have Tender Grapes* about an immigrant Norwegian farm family in Wisconsin with Edward G. Robinson and Margaret O'Brien in the lead roles.

During this fruitful period, Trumbo also wrote another novel about a bank clerk who finds a small discrepancy in the city budget and doggedly pursues its source while his bosses attempt to pin the blame on him. Coming to his aid is the spirit of the American champion of rugged individualism, General Andrew Jackson, Old Hickory himself. *The Remarkable Andrew* was also turned into a movie in 1942. While Trumbo often called *The Remarkable Andrew* the worst thing he ever wrote, the fantasy, at least in movie form, has fared well in popular opinion.

Chapter 3: Communism and Blacklisting

During this time Trumbo did not confine his writing to the movies. He was well-known around Hollywood for his support of Democratic political candidates, and put in time as the chairman of Writers for Roosevelt that took out ads in movie trade papers seeking to mobilize talent for the President's re-election campaigns. If there was an anti-fascist, pro-labor or civil rights cause being promoted around town, there was a good chance Dalton Trumbo might be involved in the demonstration.

Not that Trumbo was alone in Hollywood in his left-leaning politics. Lists of hundreds of members of "Hollywood is for FDR" were printed in the newspapers who were "men and women of the Motion Pictures Colony united by the common bond of respect for the decent administration of government who believe that Franklin Roosevelt's re-election is vital to the security of our country and its place in the post-war world." Studio heads Samuel Goldwyn and Jack Warner and the biggest star in Hollywood, Katharine Hepburn, co-chaired the committee.

In 1940, Harry Bridges, an Australian-born labor leader who organized the International Longshoremen's and Warehousemen's Union in ports along the West Coast was facing deportation as a Communist, and Trumbo attended a testimonial dinner in Bridges' honor. He then wrote a pamphlet defending Bridges that was published by the Hollywood Chapter of the League of American Writers. Bridges would lose his case and all subsequent appeals until the Supreme Court ruled in his favor in 1945. He became a United States citizen that year but the government tried again to deport him and again the Supreme Court overturned his conviction.

In 1943, Dalton Trumbo officially joined the Communist Party. There was no great revelation, no seismic shifts of dogma. As Trumbo would later relate, "Some of my best friends were Communists. And no one pressed me to join. There was really no reason to. To me, it was not a matter of great consequence. It represented no significant change in my thought or in my life." He drifted out of the party as breezily as he entered, quitting in 1948 when he got tired of driving the 85 miles to Los Angles from the Lazy T.

The government was not taking such activities as lightly. Authorities began to be worried that increasingly liberal Hollywood was actively inserting subversive messages into movies for mass Communist recruitment as early as the 1930s. In the 1940s, State Senator Jack Tenney's California Joint Fact-finding Committee on Un-American Activities began looking into these supposedly subversive plots, ignoring one basic truism of Hollywood: the only alter at which studio moguls worshipped was that of the almighty dollar. As Jack Warner once famously snorted, "If you want to send a message, use Western Union."

Besides, the United States was fighting fascism, not Communism, in World War II. The Communists were on our side. When "red hunters" went looking for actual evidence of Hollywood pro-Communist sympathies, the only pro-Russia movie they could find was *Mission to Moscow*, an anti-isolationist script that Jack Warner had produced at the request of the Roosevelt administration.

With the end of World War II and the beginning of the Cold War, however, the United States government had an excuse to ramp up the hysteria in ferreting out Hollywood radicals. The House Un-American Activities Committee (HUAC) in the United States House of Representatives that had been a specialized investigating committee called periodically since the 1930s, was made a permanent committee in 1945. The mandate of the HUAC was to investigate threats by actual subversion or propaganda that attacked "the form of government by our Constitution."

In 1947, the HUAC convened nine days of hearings poking for Communist influences in the motion picture industry. Subpoenas were issued throughout Hollywood to producers, directors, actors and, most pervasively, the individuals who put words into the movies, screenwriters. At first, the industry defied the HUAC and the first witnesses read statements ridiculing the "witch hunt" but negative publicity forced industry insiders to begin addressing the charges against them.

There was little tangible evidence to identify a Hollywood Communist or even define what that meant. Dalton Trumbo's name first came up during testimony from Lela Rogers, the mother of Ginger Rogers. She told the committee that, against her daughter's will, she had been compelled to speak Trumbo's subversive line "share and share alike, that's democracy."

Some of the witnesses gave the HUAC what they wanted. Walt Disney identified the Communist threat in Hollywood as a serious matter. Ronald Reagan, president of the Screen Actors Guild, named several members of his union who held Communist sympathies. Fifty-seven year old actor Adolphe Menjou, who had been nominated for an Academy Award in 1931's *The Front Page*, testified that a Communist is "anyone attending a meeting at which Paul Robeson appears - and applauds!"

Other testimony served only to highlight the lunacy of the proceedings. Rogers and Oliver Carlson, a professor at the University of California, were subpoenaed because they were so-called "veteran detectors of Communism in the films." Gary Cooper was summoned to Capitol Hill only to explain his appearance in Communist leaflets in Italy that quoted him as saying in a speech before a crowd of 90,000 Communists in Philadelphia, "In our days it is the greatest honor to be a Communist." In a slow take, either for dramatic effect or contemplating the unlikelihood of 90,000 Communists gathering for a speech on American streets, Cooper grinned and replied, "Well, that 90,000 audience is a little tough to disregard - but it is not true."

The centerpiece of the hearings was 19 witnesses - the Unfriendly 19 - who declared they would not be giving any evidence to the HUAC. Eleven, all screenwriters, were issued summons to appear before the committee. One, Bertolt Brecht, who was a German national and a refugee from Adolf Hitler's regime, capitulated. He had arrived in America two days before the raid on Pearl Harbor and took out his first citizenship papers the day following the Japanese bombing. He affirmed in a thick German accent that he had not only been to Moscow, but he had good friends who were Russians, and had written words to music composed by Communist Hanns Eisler. But no, he was not a Communist. Chairman J. Parnell Thomas thanked Brecht for his testimony.

Things would not proceed as smoothly with the remaining ten witnesses. Dalton Trumbo was the second of the ten called before the committee; when sworn in he settled behind the table between lawyers Robert Kenny and Bartley Crum. He navigated through two questions from chief investigator Robert E. Stripling - his name and place of birth - before the interrogation went off the rails. After identifying his occupation as a writer, Trumbo attempted to introduce statements from Henry H. Arnold, the only Air Force general to hold five-star rank and the only person to hold a five-star rank in two different U.S. military services, and others testifying to his character. The statements were dismissed as not relevant.

Trumbo was asked if he was a member of the Screen Writers Guild. Trumbo replied that he could not answer yes or no since "the rights of American labor to secrecy as to membership in a union or guild have long been held inviolate." Getting nowhere, Stripling moved on to his main question: "Are you now, or have you ever been, a member of the Communist Party?"

Trumbo had three avenues of response. He could deny ever being a Communist, knowing that the HUAC had a plump dossier of his years on the fringe of Communist-related activities. In fact Stripling held in front of him a folder containing a document nine pages long of single-spaced accusations entitled "Communist Affiliations of Dalton Trumbo." Most of it was circumstantial nonsense; Trumbo had expressed support for political candidates who were suspected Communists, Trumbo had sold artwork at a Hollywood auction to benefit an American Marxist magazine called the New Masses, Trumbo had given a speech at a Los Angeles Peace Rally for an organization that later decried Franklin Roosevelt as a warmonger, his name was on the letterhead of the American Youth for Democracy, he was a contributing sponsor of the Sleepy Lagoon Defense that was three degrees removed from the Communist Party's legal eagles.

Some of the "evidence" even contradicted itself. Trumbo was cited for being a sponsor of the Artists' Front to Win the War and authoring "An Open Letter to the American People" imploring citizens in 1942 to wire President Roosevelt to open a second front in the war. Apparently Roosevelt could come in the shape of a warmonger or a lead-footed war leader. If Trumbo was even minimally involved in all the Communist activities the government accused him of, it would have quite a magic feat to become one of Hollywood's highest paid scriptwriters, earning an estimated $100,000 a year. But the government dossier also contained Party Card 47187, a Communist registration card from 1944 belonging to "Dalt T., 620 Beverly Drive, Los Angeles."

So claiming he was never a member of the Communist Party was one pathway closed to Trumbo. He could also answer "yes" and almost certainly end his career. He could also state that, yes, he had been a Communist Party member at one time but had since renounced all ties to return to the patriotic fold. Such an admission was nearly always met with clemency.

In the end, Trumbo chose none of the three options. He did not refuse to answer the question which would be a direct contempt of Congress, but he protested the right for the government to even ask the question as a violation of the First Amendment right of free speech and invasion into a person's private life. Trumbo was eventually dismissed from the hearing room. The following eight witnesses all took the same tactic.

The nine days of hearings by the House on Un-American Activities Committee covered neither side in glory. The government politicians were exposed mostly as bungling publicity seekers, Hollywood stars were shown as stool pigeons saving their own skins, the recalcitrant screenwriters were looked on as principled Communists, and Hollywood producers were revealed for what everyone knew they were: executives only interested in the bottom line. Americans, if they cared at all, were left to grapple with a fundamental question: is it un-American to ask if someone is a Communist or is it un-American to refuse to answer?

As it turned out that was a hypothetical question for everyone except the ten screenwriters who had refused to provide evidence. A month after the hearings ended, the United States House of Representatives voted 346 to 17 to issue citations against the "Hollywood Ten" for contempt of Congress. Wasting no time, the next day the Motion Picture Association of America said that, effective immediately, all ten screenwriters were off the payroll and none would be re-hired until such time as that individual had been cleared of contempt charges and made sworn statements that he was not a Communist. On November 25, 1947, Hollywood had its first official blacklist.

Chapter 4: Life On The Blacklist

In 1948 the Hollywood Ten - Alvah Bessie, Herbert Biberman, Lester Cole, Edward Dmytryk, Ring Lardner Jr., John Howard Lawson, Albert Maltz, Samuel Ornitz, Robert Adrian Scott, and Dalton Trumbo - were all convicted of contempt and sentenced to serve one year in the federal penitentiary. As the appeals process began, Trumbo began pioneering a "blacklist black market" in order to continue providing for his family and to cover mounting legal fees.

In 1948 and 1949 he wrote five original screenplays. Marketing the scripts to studios through friends in the industry, Trumbo was able to sell two for $40,000 each, one for $35,000 and one for $11,000. One failed to sell. In each case, the "front" that provided the name kept one-third of the money and passed along two-thirds to Trumbo, directed toward an account in his wife's name. The whole sum would be reported on the front's income tax, the amount remitted to Mrs. Trumbo deducted as payment for literary services, and all money received by the Trumbos reported on their income tax so as to satisfy all legalities.

As Trumbo wrote to a friend in proposing such an arrangement, "If you have any moral compunctions about such a procedure in relation to motion pictures, please forget them. Hollywood is a vast whorehouse, and any scheme by which tolerably honest men can abstract money from it for their own purposes is more than praiseworthy."

The first of the four stories Trumbo sold during his first years on the blacklist was Gun Crazy, using screenwriter Millard Kaufman, who had just introduced the cartoon character of the nearsighted Mr. Magoo, as his front. Gun Crazy has been acclaimed as one of the great film noir movies with its story of an amoral desperado couple on the lam reminiscent of Bonnie and Clyde with Laurie, the female protagonist, the one who is fascinated with firearms. More important than the movie's success to Trumbo was the fact that brothers Frank and Maurice King produced the film, and they would become regular customers during his blacklisted period.

In 1949 Trumbo also published a 40-page pamphlet called "The Time Of The Toad: A Study Of Inquisition In America By One Of The Hollywood Ten", the title being taken from French writer Emile Zola's condemnation of public indifference to the political scandals that were ripping France asunder in the late 19th century. Trumbo argued that it was not the shrill cries of those seeking to destroy freedom that he was concerned with. Instead he feared "the others - the silent ones, the contented, the alienated, the frightened, the acquiescent."

Meanwhile, the Hollywood blacklist continued to grow. The Hollywood Ten's legal team chose to pursue absolute victory in support of ideals rather than leniency, and lost all appeals. To present their case before the United States Supreme Court, the legal team filed an advocacy brief with the names of 204 Hollywood professionals. Not only did the Supreme Court decline to review the case of the Hollywood Ten, but 84 who signed the brief were added to the industry blacklist.

Dalton Trumbo entered the Federal Correctional Institute in Ashland, Kentucky in June of 1950. Members of the Hollywood Ten were sent to different prisons around the country. In Danbury, Connecticut, Ring Lardner, Jr. had a reunion of sorts with Parnell Thomas. The red-baiting chairman of the House Un-American Activities Committee had been imprisoned for stuffing his Congressional payroll with non-existent employees.

Trumbo spent ten months incarcerated, devoting his time to his serious writing, sending humorous letters to his family to keep their spirits buoyant (he signed the missives with his Prisoner Number, 7551), and reading the complete 1,225 pages of Leo Tolstoy's *War and Peace*. He was assigned a prison detail to work as a clerk in a storeroom which put a typewriter at his disposal and he was able to write a screenplay which he later sold on the black market.

As he later wrote about his time at Ashland: "It was a place of quality as evidenced by the fact that the head librarian was a Congressman there for a felony called taking a bribe, whereas I was there for a misdemeanor called contempt of Congress. Try as I might I could not repent of the crime of contempt for an idiotic Congress." After he was released from jail he returned to Los Angeles where, several months shy of his 46th birthday and in the prime earning years of his career, Dalton Trumbo's name was etched permanently on the Hollywood blacklist.

Still, Trumbo was better off than most who were blacklisted. Actors could not change their faces and directors could not relay instructions to the set via walkie-talkies. Many careers were ruined. In 1951 the House Un-American Activities Committee launched a second investigation aimed at Communism in Hollywood. Whereas the committee that corralled the Hollywood Ten was instigated under a Republican Congress, this second HUAC was green-lighted by a Democratic-controlled legislature under a Democratic President. This second version of Hollywood cleansing was notably lacking in any investigative camouflage. The political sympathies of the witnesses called was public knowledge. Instead, this time the witnesses were expected to express regrets about past activity and demonstrate now-proud patriotism by providing the names of comrades.

Some agreed with the committee that there was a Communist influence in Hollywood and named names. Most famously in this small group was Elia Kazan who walked out of the hearings to direct award-winning movies in the next few years like On the Waterfront and East of Eden. A rare few, like Lucille Ball, were allowed to respond with nonsensical explanations and given a pass.

Two out of three of those called were unfriendly witnesses who defied the HUAC and suffered the consequences of blacklisting. Sam Jaffe had been a successful actor for years and had been nominated just a year earlier for his turn as Doc Erwin Riedenschneider in The Asphalt Jungle. After his testimony, the 60-year old Jaffe was reduced to teaching high school math and living with his sisters. He would not return to Hollywood for six years.

Lionel Stander was born in the Bronx and was known in the movies for his gravelly voice as he became the most highly paid character actor in Hollywood. Off the set he was active in the Screen Actors Guild, raised money for the anti-fascists in Spain, and helped organize a lettuce strike in the Salinas Valley. When Stander testified, he assured the committee that he never considered joining the Communist Party because he was much further left than that. Stander's radical beliefs had kept him off of major studio lots for years; now he was blacklisted by all of Hollywood. He went to New York, became a stockbroker on Wall Street and worked in local theater. Stander found starring roles in European movies and eventually returned to Hollywood to handle the chauffeur duties on Robert Wagner and Stephanie Power's long-running television show, Hart to Hart, in the 1980s.

But Jaffe and Stander were rare exceptions of blacklisted outcasts who found Hollywood work again. It is estimated that no more than 10 percent of those blacklisted ever regained their Hollywood careers. Most of those were screenwriters; about a quarter were actors. Trumbo managed to avoid the terminal fate of blacklisting because he had skills that were always in demand in the movie business: he could write fast and efficiently. Trumbo would turn in a clean, 150-page screenplay in a week. He started with the dialogue and then fleshed out the plot with descriptions and action.

Upon arriving back in Los Angeles, however, Trumbo discovered that most of the friends who helped sherpa black market scripts for him before he went to jail had left town or been blacklisted themselves. Even his agent had been forced out of business by the impact of the Hollywood blacklist. Trumbo began making discreet inquiries, aware that his future paychecks would be a fraction of those he was cashing when he could command $75,000 for a script. His first contact was the King Brothers, letting them know he was available to work on screenplays for their independent production company. They sent over several short stories and a novel to consider.

The depleted Trumbo bank account was not the only effect of the blacklist. The Hollywood lifestyle and old friends were also closed off to Dalton and Cleo. Trumbo began to explore his options to move away from southern California. He dismissed New York City as too expensive and Europe was out of the question since, as a convicted felon, he could not obtain a passport. Trumbo began investigating Mexico where some blacklisted writers had already moved, most notably Gordon Kahn, screenwriter of over 40 movies including uncredited work on The African Queen and All Quiet on the Western Front. Kahn had lobbied publicly for the freedom of the Hollywood Ten and fled to Mexico when he was called to appear before the second House on Un-American Activities Committee.

Trumbo learned from Kahn that the living expenses in Mexico City were a pittance compared to Los Angeles, and that there was a good American school in the city. Furthermore, he was still close enough to market his scripts in Hollywood and there was work to be had in the Mexican film industry. All the arguments for moving out of the country were lining up, save one.

Rather than be stranded alone in a foreign country, Trumbo determined that the move could not be executed without Canadian-born screenwriter Hugo Butler and his wife, actress Jean Rouverol. The two families were close and as Trumbo pointed out, that bond would sustain the families in a strange land. Trumbo wrote Butler that, "We can mutually spur each other on to work. The fact is that in movies and originals, two minds often strike sparks, provided both are hard enough, as I think is the case. We could provide for each other and broods as a sort of mutual aid society in time of need or other harassment." When Butler's name began being bandied about by the new HUAC in Washington, he needed little more persuasion.

In 1952, the Lazy T Ranch was sold and the Trumbos and Butlers gathered in San Diego. They drove east across Arizona and New Mexico and entered Mexico and Ciudad Juarez through El Paso. Once in Mexico City, Hollywood Ten members Ring Lardner, Jr. and Albert Maltz would join the tight-knit community of screenwriters in exile, as would numbers of other writers and poets during the Cold War of the 1950s.

The Americans traveled frequently about the countryside, absorbing Mexican culture at historical sites and festivals. Some, like Cleo Trumbo and the Butlers, took Spanish lessons to learn the language of their new country. Dalton Trumbo had no intention of following their lead and insisted on speaking English, while acknowledging the well-intended efforts of his compatriots.

In his time on the blacklist, Trumbo would write some 30 screenplays under at least 13 different names, doing some of the best work of his career at drastically reduced wages. One of the first scripts he wrote while in Mexico City was about a bored princess who slips out of her cloistered castle during a goodwill tour of Europe, and spends the night experiencing Rome and falling in love with Gregory Peck. *Roman Holiday* was delivered to Hollywood and director William Wyler by Trumbo's friend, Ian McLellan Hunter.

Roman Holiday was released in 1953 and became a much-beloved hit. It has charmed audiences for more than half a century as one of Hollywood's favorite movies. In 1954 Audrey Hepburn won the Oscar for her film debut as Princess Anne and Edith Head won for her costume designs on the movie that was shot entirely in Rome. *Roman Holiday* also won the Academy Award for Best Writing, Motion Picture Story. Ian McLellan Hunter accepted the golden statuette on Oscar night. Hunter would always acknowledge to friends that because the Academy Award was for story it was wholly Trumbo's prize; had it been for screenwriting on which Hunter worked, he could have convinced himself to deserving some of the credit.

Dalton Trumbo had his screenwriting fee but no recognition beyond what a select few insiders knew. In 2011, friends Chris Trumbo and Tim Hunter, sons of the writers, successfully lobbied to restore Dalton Trumbo's screenplay credit to the venerable film classic. Prints of *Roman Holiday* now read:

Screenplay by Dalton Trumbo and Ian McLellan Hunter and John Dighton

Story by Dalton Trumbo

While in Mexico City, Hugo Butler became enthralled with the national sport of bullfighting. He started going to the local arenas every Sunday and took to reading about the lore and meaning of the exhibitions. All of this was lost on Trumbo, especially after the first fight he attended a bullfight that ended in a bungled and unnecessarily cruel kill.

Butler argued that, since we kill cows for meat all the time, how did it matter how the act was accomplished? Trumbo, who had a few cows and bulls on the Lazy T, did not see it Butler's way, even after his friend pointed out that the bull was not a passive victim of slaughter but could extract revenge on his attacker and, if he fought bravely enough, might even win an indulto, or pardon, from the crowd. Trumbo even saw an indulto given after a fight he and Butler witnessed.

The two never found common ground on the subject of Mexican bullfighting but Trumbo did begin to piece together a story about a boy and a bull. Leonardo is a young boy who lives on a ranch where his father raises bulls for the owner to fight. Leonardo becomes attached to one bull named Gitano and convinces the owner to keep him around as a stud bull. But the owner dies and Gitano gets auctioned off as the ranch is divided. Leonardo is left to take a desperate journey to track down Gitano and save his life.

In May of 1952, Trumbo traveled to Los Angeles to pitch the storyline for *The Boy and the Bull* personally to the King Brothers. Trumbo was never sentimental about his movie work; in his mind stories were not designed to make motion pictures, they were only designed to sell to studios. His Mexican bull tale was no exception. If the King Brothers were not interested enough to advance him money, he was more than prepared to abandon the project.

The King Brothers did like Trumbo's bullfighting story but not enough to send him back to Mexico with a check. Enough concessions and agreements were made on a handshake, however, that Trumbo agreed to write the screenplay and the King Brothers agreed to his price if they liked it. That was enough for Trumbo to complete the script on speculation; he returned to Mexico City, read books on bullfighting, and wrote the screenplay.

Trumbo worked on a panoply of scripts while in exile, completing 18 in all. There was *Carnival*, a melodrama set in an American circus touring Germany; *They Were So Young*, the story of a Rio de Janeiro model agency used as a front for the South American sex slave trade; and *The Court Martial of Billy Mitchell*, the dramatization of the American general fighting for the modernization of his country's air force. Meanwhile, the Mexican experience was growing old for Trumbo.

In 1954, after two years in Mexico City, the Trumbos moved back to California, settling in the Highland Park neighborhood of Northeast Los Angeles. The Butlers, always more enamored of Mexico, would stay another eleven years. By this time Trumbo had been on the Hollywood blacklist for almost seven years and the Red Scare was at its zenith with Wisconsin Senator Joseph McCarthy convening hearings intended to smoke out secret Communists from the United States Army.

The government may have been hunting Communists under different rocks but the atmosphere in Hollywood was still poisoned. Mitzi Trumbo was drummed out of the Blue Birds (young Campfire Girls) for her father's background, and ostracized so severely in elementary school that Trumbo was forced to write letters to the school's officials accusing them of receiving the happy little girl he was sending out of the house each day, and returning a destroyed human being at the end of the day. Christopher Trumbo was denied an academic award in high school for being a member of the Trumbo family.

Trumbo continued writing at a breakneck pace and opened bank accounts in different names around town to conceal his identity. Bank clerks were given rewards for providing information on anyone suspected of subversive activities, so Trumbo never signed any checks in his own name. Of course, he could never resist tweaking the authorities. The checking account he opened in nearby Pasadena at the United States National Bank on Colorado Avenue was in the names of James and Dorothy Bonham. Any obsessive Trumbo watchers may have detected the surname was the same as his father's middle name and the lead character in his novel Johnny Got His Gun.

Meanwhile, McCarthy's tactics in attacking the United States Army were being unveiled as "partial truth and innuendo." McCarthy became ever more virulent in the face of charges against him as support for his histrionics began to erode. On December 2, 1954, the United States Senate voted to censure McCarthy by a mostly non-partisan vote of 67-22. Americans were beginning to worry less about ghost Communists in their military and on their movie screens, and more about the real Communists in the Soviet Union that had been exploding nuclear bombs since 1949.

The blacklist in Hollywood was continuing to go strong, however, fueled by innuendo that often appeared in influential industry columns by Walter Winchell and Hedda Hopper. A small crack in the blacklist stonewall appeared in 1954, when actor John Ireland sued advertising agency Young & Rubicam for ordering him off a television series due to a suggestion he was less than patriotic. The agency settled out of court in an admission the industry had routinely threatened show business employees based on rumors without substance. From that point on, Ireland's name appeared in the gossip columns connected to young starlets like Tuesday Weld and Natalie Wood rather than Communists.

Trumbo even briefly rejoined the Communist Party in 1954 as a token gesture of support for 14 officials in California who were convicted under the terms of the Alien Registration Act of 1940, more widely known as the Smith Act. When the convictions were overturned and the defendants set free, Trumbo severed ties to the Communists again.

Back in Hollywood, the King Brothers had indeed been pleased with the bullfighting screenplay that Trumbo had delivered from Mexico. They found Irving Rapper, an English-born American director who had been a busy contract director for Warner Brothers, to helm the film. Rapper's *One Foot in Heaven* from 1941 had been nominated for a Best Picture Oscar. For the role of Leonardo, the Kings cast Michel Ray, the son of an English mother and Brazilian father who had made his film debut in *The Divided Heart* when he was ten years old in 1954. The role called for a young boy who could ski, and Ray had learned how to ski when very young as a school boy in Switzerland. He had no similar bullfighting qualifications for *The Boy and the Bull.*

When he reached the age of 18 in 1962, Ray
would quit acting and go to school at Harvard.
He skied for the British Olympic team in the
1968 Winter Games in Grenoble, France, and
competed in both the 1972 and 1976 Olympics in
the luge. By that time, he had made millions of
dollars as an investment banker. He would
marry his childhood friend Charlene Heineken
who was heir to the Dutch brewing
conglomerate, the controlling interest to which
the couple would inherit in 2002. So the young
actor had a future as a billionaire many times
over, but in the 1950s he was still just a child
actor working with a bull on sets in Mexico.

The film from King Brothers Productions was
released on October 26, 1956. It had a new name,
The Brave One, and its writer was Robert Rich, a
name made up by Dalton Trumbo. The movie
had no identifiable stars and featured an
unfamiliar and possibly difficult subject. But *The
Brave One* found an audience and surprisingly
garnered three Academy Award nominations in
1957: Best Film Editing, Best Sound Recording
and Best Motion Picture Story.

The Brave One lost the first two categories and faced stiff competition in the writing category. It was up against *The Eddy Duchin Story*, a biopic about the band leader and pianist with Tyrone Power in the lead; *High Society* with its high-octane stars Frank Sinatra, Grace Kelly and Bing Crosby; *The Proud and the Beautiful* by celebrated French philosopher Jean-Paul Sartre; and the Italian film *Umberto D.* written by honored screen veteran Cesare Zavattini.

At the RKO Pantage Theatre in Hollywood on the night of the 29th Academy Awards, English actress and multiple Oscar nominee Deborah Kerr read the list of contenders for Best Motion Picture Story, opened the envelope and read the name of the winner written on the card. The winner was...Robert Rich. Then, nothing. As the audience applauded no one showed up on stage to accept the Oscar, the only time an Academy Award went unclaimed at the ceremonies. Jesse Lasky Jr., vice president of the Writers Guild, swept into the void to gather up the statuette and relieve Ms. Kerr's growing discomfort. "Mr. Rich is right now at the hospital, waiting for his wife to give birth," he explained to the befuddled audience.

The Oscar win by an unknown writer with no previous screen credits against such august competition was a juicy story, and one reporter was sent after the mysterious Robert Rich for a quote and an exclusive. He checked every maternity ward in Los Angeles County but could not find a Mrs. Robert Rich in any of them. Meanwhile, alleged Robert Riches were milling about threatening lawsuits against the King Brothers for stealing their stories. Before the situation spiraled out of control, Frank King revealed for the record that the story author was the blacklisted writer, Dalton Trumbo.

So Hollywood maintained a blacklist but Hollywood was using scripts by blacklisted writers and even giving them awards. Trumbo wasted no time in ridiculing the hypocritical and harmful blacklist. He gave interviews to anyone who asked and probably to some who did not. He appeared on television to debate defenders of the blacklist. The phantom Oscar winner made a standing offer that he would gladly write a movie for any Hollywood producer free of charge in exchange for placing his name on the credits.

After that, fissures began to break the blacklist apart in television. Alfred Hitchock hired blacklisted actor Norman Lloyd to work on his CBS anthology series, Alfred Hitchcock Presents, later in 1957. At holiday time in 1958, the names of Ruth McKenney, a Communist writer, and blacklisted Edward Chodorov appeared on a live production of Wonderful Time on CBS.

On January 20, 1960 director Otto Preminger released a statement announcing that Dalton Trumbo would be listed as screenwriter on his yet to be released film *Exodus*, with Paul Newman starring in the story of the founding of Israel. The novel by Leon Uris, as Trumbo remembered, "weighed 14 pounds and had 390 characters." Preminger needed the screenplay in three weeks, beginning on December 16. Trumbo liked to relate the tale of how the director showed up at his house on Christmas Eve, and practically opened the presents himself to move holiday proceedings along quicker.

Before *Exodus* would premiere, on October 7, 1960 Stanley Kubrick's sprawling epic of a slave rebellion in ancient Greece, Spartacus, opened. Producer and star Kirk Douglas insisted that Dalton Trumbo's name appear as screenwriter. It was the first time a blacklisted writer's name appeared on a Hollywood motion picture. Just like that, the blacklist was over.

Chapter 5: Later Life

In 1960, Dalton Trumbo was in his 55th year. He had been deemed unemployable by Hollywood for 13 years and denied the biggest paychecks of his career. He had done some of his best work on the blacklist and, even though there were no gold statuettes on his mantel, had won two Academy Awards.

As Trumbo's name returned to the screen the contributions of other blacklisted writers in the 1950s began to come to light. Nedrick Young had written the screenplay for Elvis Presley's *Jailhouse Rock* and for Stanley Kramer's *The Defiant Ones* that earned an Oscar for Best Writing Written Directly for the Screen in 1959. Blacklisted writers Carl Foreman and Michael Wilson had both gone uncredited for their work on *The Bridge on the River Kwai* that won seven Oscars at the 1958 Academy Awards, including one for Best Writing on a Screenplay Based on Material from Another Medium.

The Writers Guild would pursue the correction of movie credits from the Hollywood blacklist era for the next half-century, but in the meantime, writers were once again taking calls from the studios. No one was in a more enviable position entering the post-blacklist era than Trumbo. In addition to his two Academy Awards, *Spartacus* had become the biggest moneymaker in the history of Universal Studios.

The film reached the top of the box office, despite it being a period piece with a running time of more than three hours and attacks against the production because of Trumbo. The American Legion urged its members to stay away from the movie and Hollywood columnist Hedda Hooper minced no words when she wrote, ""The story was sold to Universal from a book written by a commie (Howard Fast) and the screen script was written by a commie, so don't go to see it." As the 1960s dawned, few were listening to such rhetoric any more.

When Otto Preminger released *Exodus* on December 15, 1960 it was even longer, clocking in at just a few ticks under three and a half hours. *Exodus* was another moneymaker and Trumbo knew he would never need to sign a contract with a studio again. In a letter to the King Brothers, he allowed that he would do a picture a year for them if they so chose, but his days of working on a term contract were over.

Meanwhile, Hollywood still had not released quite all the work Trumbo had written under the cloud of the blacklist. While Spartacus was still in post-production, Douglas, who always enjoyed Trumbo's scripts, hired him again to adapt Howard Rigsby's novel *Sundown at Crazy Horse* for the movies. The story involves a man wanted for murder pursued by a sheriff who crosses into Mexico and heads for the ranch of a former lover where he falls for her daughter. The movie, starring Universal's top box office idol Rock Hudson opposite Douglas, was shot completely in Mexico and brought in on time in April of 1960 but would not be released until June of 1961, arriving in theaters as *The Last Sunset*.

The Last Sunset was generally dismissed as television fare, but Douglas and Trumbo teamed up for a third time, to film an adaption of Edward Abbey's 1956 novel *The Brave Cowboy: An Old Tale in a New Time*. Abbey's tale follows an aging cowboy railing against the loss of his independent way of life in the New West. The veteran of the range wars gets himself tossed into jail to help a friend unjustly sentenced to escape. In the end, the cowboy on horseback is chased across the desert by cars and helicopters.

The movie was reportedly shot scene-for-scene from Trumbo's script, and Douglas reported that he found the writer's screenplay so perfect he did not change a single word of it. Of the 75 movies Kirk Douglas made in a 60-year career, he repeatedly said this was his favorite. It was also the only time he ever acted or produced a movie where the screenplay was "one draft, no revisions."

Douglas argued with Universal Studios about the title (Douglas wanted to call it *The Last Cowboy*) and requested that it be released into art houses to build word of mouth. The studio heads saw it as just another Western, slapped the name *Lonely Are the Brave* on it and dumped it in theaters without promotional support in the summer of 1962, then considered a wasteland for movie-going.

Lonely Are the Brave came and went with barely a whimper, generating far less money than Douglas and Trumbo's first collaboration two years earlier. It did not escape complete notice, however. The next year, Kirk Douglas was nominated for a Best Foreign Actor Award by the British Academy of Film and Television Arts. In the ensuing years, many have concurred with Douglas and rank *Lonely Are the Brave* among the best Westerns ever made; it certainly stands alongside the best of Dalton Trumbo's screenplays.

At this point, Trumbo was entering a new phase in his career. The studio system was breaking down in Hollywood, and the movies no longer required an assembly line of B picture scripts that Trumbo had specialized in producing while he was blacklisted and when he was first making a name for himself. Besides, with the blacklist broken, he no longer had to work three times as hard to earn but a fraction of his going rate. Accordingly, as Trumbo approached his 60th birthday, his working pace slackened, and he began to take breaks from his screenwriting routine.

Trumbo's work would not appear on the screen again until 1965. The project was The Sandpiper starring Hollywood's most talked about couple, Elizabeth Taylor and Richard Burton. MGM was bringing the gossip magnets together for the third time, and it was not the only news-making pairing attached to the picture. Trumbo co-wrote the screenplay with his fellow blacklisted Academy Award-winning friend, Michael Wilson. In their banishment, the two had teamed up on occasion but this was the only time the two famous "Communist" writers worked together in the sunlight of the open era.

The need to entertain was not so critical for Trumbo and Wilson in their post-blacklist writing as it had been in their early days. Message-laden speeches were coming from the mouths of their characters more often in the 1960s which came out as pretentious in *The Sandpiper*. The movie was ravaged by critics but audiences only had eyes for Liz and Dick, and the movie made money for all involved. It won an Academy Award in 1966 but it was for its evergreen theme song, "The Shadow of Your Smile," written by Johnny Mandel and Paul Francis Webster.

Under attack by the widespread adoption of television, Hollywood fought back by producing what could never be replicated on the small screen: sprawling epics. Trumbo got the call to adapt James Michener's 937-page story of *Hawaii* for the big screen. Michener's exhaustively researched best-seller was translated into 32 languages, and fans eagerly anticipated its arrival on the screen.

Director Fred Zinnemann and Trumbo wanted to divide the brawny story into two separate movies. When the United Artists studio balked, Zinnemann bailed and let *Hawaii* sail on without him. It would be a rocky road for replacement director George Roy Hill, who was reportedly fired and re-hired three times as the project lurched towards completion. Even by truncating several hundred years of narrative and focusing only on a single chapter when the first Christian missionaries came to Hawaii, Trumbo's script for the movie would last more than three hours.

The budget for the ambitious production climbed to ten million dollars and was filmed on location in Hawaii, Norway, Tahiti and New England. When *Hawaii* swept into theaters in 1966, it was generally considered to be a disappointment, but at Oscar time in 1967 the film garnered seven nominations, the most of any picture Dalton Trumbo was connected with outside of *Roman Holiday*. None of the nominations was for writing, however. Four years later, the neglected portions of Michener's story were filmed in a sequel called *The Hawaiians* but none of those involved in the original were involved.

Even as *Hawaii* was being feted at the Oscar ceremonies in 1967, Hollywood was undergoing seismic changes. The bloated, big-budget epics were being pushed aside in favor of smaller, culturally topical movies. Included on the list of Best Picture nominees in 1968 would be movies like *The Graduate* with Dustin Hoffman rejecting the trappings of his conventional upbringing; In *The Heat of the Night* where Sidney Poitier's black Philadelphia detective becomes involved in Sheriff Rod Steiger's murder investigation in a racist Mississippi town; *Guess Who's Coming to Dinner* with open-minded Katharine Hepburn and Spencer Tracy reacting to their daughter's interracial romance; and *Bonnie and Clyde* where the violence and raw sexuality challenged just about every taboo in Hollywood. Where the movie industry was once the fiefdom of the studio moguls, it was rapidly transforming into a director's medium. Dalton Trumbo began in the film business in the 1930s in a studio screenplay factory taking home $75 a week. He would work the final years of his career in the New Hollywood.

Trumbo's first steps in the New Hollywood were halting ones. His source material had the finest literary pedigree; he was hired to write the screenplay for Bernard Malamud's *The Fixer*. Based on the true story of a Jewish bricklayer in Czarist Russia who refuses to admit to a murder he did not commit, Malamud won both a National Book Award and a Pulitzer Prize for the novel in 1967.

The director attached to the project was first rate as well. John Frankenheimer was acclaimed for such socially conscious films as *The Manchurian Candidate* about political brainwashing; *Seven Days in May* about nuclear threat in the Cold War; and *The Train* with Burt Lancaster and French resistance fighters trying to stop the country's finest artworks from being spirited out of the country by Germans during World War II.

The Fixer, produced by the Metro-Goldwyn-Mayer's British Studios, was shot on location entirely in Hungary, the first American-connected movie to be filmed entirely in a Communist country. Despite the high-powered connections, Trumbo threw himself into the work slowly. Comedian Steve Martin, then 23 years old and writing on The Smothers Brothers Comedy Hour was dating Trumbo's daughter Mitzi at the time and recalled her telling him about her father's assignment with *The Fixer*: "He's got a screenplay due in four days and he hasn't started it yet."

Trumbo and his screenplay showed up in Hungary where he was involved in every day of the shooting. When Frankenheimer found out that one of the requirements for using Hungarian crew and supplies was also using Hungarian actors, Trumbo wrote in improvised non-speaking parts. When they needed something as simple as nails, they could not simply be bought but had to be requisitioned from the government, a process that would take days. The shooting schedule went way too long and the movie was way too long. The final cut of the movie, even at more than two hours, left much of the backstory and several critical scenes on the editing room floor. The first of many harsh reviews for Frankenheimer came from Trumbo himself who wrote the whipsawn director a scathing five-page letter after he was shown a rough cut.

For his next project Dalton Trumbo would have an author he knew intimately and a director who would adhere to his every demand: World Entertainment hired him to direct the film version of his 1939 novel *Johnny Got His Gun*. Since its publication thirty years earlier Trumbo's novel had been seized upon by the Beat Generation and protest singers in the 1960s. The character in Bob Dylan's "John Brown" who returns to his mother blinded and injured from war is in homage to *Johnny Got His Gun*.

Spanish director Luis Buñuel and Trumbo banged out a script from the novel in the 1960s but nothing came of the project. By the end of the decade, the Vietnam War was at its height. Protests against the war had helped forced Lyndon Johnson from office, and were growing louder every day. The time seemed right for an anti-war movie in the New Hollywood.

Trumbo harbored no illusions about making his directorial debut at the age of 66. "I finally had to direct the damned thing myself," he once said to film critic Roger Ebert, "because I was old enough to have been there, to remember what it was like. I'm older than everybody. I'm even older than Preminger."

Universal casting scouts found a young 19-year old actor named Timothy Bottoms in a local stage production of *Romeo and Juliet* and gave him the lead role of Joe Bonham with no prior movie experience. Veteran actor Jason Robards, who had not yet won his two Oscars, signed on to play Joe's father and Marsha Hunt was cast as his mother. Hunt had made her first movie the same year Trumbo got his first full-time Hollywood writing job, and had over 100 acting credits but somehow had never appeared in a Trumbo-penned movie. A vocal supporter of free speech, Hunt's name ended up in a pamphlet called "Red Channels" in the 1950s and she spent part of the decade blacklisted as well. Canadian actor Donald Sutherland, coming off his turn as Hawkeye Pierce in Robert Altman's MASH, was also in the *Johnny Got His Gun* ensemble cast.

In filming his story Trumbo never showed Joe's face directly on camera and sheets always covered his missing limbs. To differentiate between the reality of Joe's tortured present and the dreams of his former life, Trumbo used the directorial trick of filming the hospital scenes in black and white and the flashbacks and fantasies in color. In a climax that he had not used in his novel Trumbo created a final scene where a nurse attempts to grant Joe's wish to die by blocking his breathing tube but she is stopped by her supervisor before the mercy deed can be completed. The picture ends with Joe helplessly pleading "S.O.S. Help me." The conclusion led some to look at *Johnny Got His Gun* not so much as an anti-war movie but as a pro-life statement.

In May of 1971 *Johnny Got His Gun* was entered in the 24th annual Cannes Film Festival in Cannes, France, considered to be the French equivalent of the Academy Awards. The movie won the Grand Prix Award, the second most prestigious prize in the festival after the Palme d'Or. It also captured a FIPRESCI Award from the International Federation of Film Critics.

Johnny Got His Gun met with a similar critical reception when it debuted in the United States later that month (Ebert gave the movie four stars out of four). But the movie never reached the wide audience its supporters believed it deserved. The film's money men got tangled up in quarrels, and the distribution by New York-based Cinemation Industries was bungled as well. Started in 1965, the firm became best known for distributing exploitation films and after the business went bankrupt in 1975, founder Jerry Gross was next seen working behind the counter at a 7-11 convenience store.

At awards season in 1972, *Johnny Got His Gun* was ignored at the Academy Awards but Trumbo was nominated for a Best Drama award by the Writers Guild of America. Bottoms had followed up his first film with another lead role in Peter Bogdanovich's landmark film, *The Last Picture Show*, a depiction of a dying West Texas town. With one of the strongest one-two movie debuts in Hollywood history, Bottoms was nominated for Best New Male Star at the Golden Globes, but somehow lost out to Desi Arnaz, Jr.

Dalton Trumbo may have sent John Frankenheimer the "most scathing" letter he had ever received after *The Fixer* was finished in 1968 but the director did not hesitate to hire the screenwriter later that year when he bought the rights to Joseph Kessel's novel *The Horsemen* for $150,000. Kessel's story was nominally about the Afghani sport of buzkashi, a sort of no-rules polo where the riders dragged around a headless goat carcass, but was more deeply about the character of the men who played the game.

Shooting was delayed by star Omar Sharif's other commitments, and then by difficulty in filming on location in Spain and Afghanistan. Frankenheimer was crafting a three-hour epic with 1,500 extras better suited for a decade earlier. When Columbia Studio demanded an exhibitor-friendly 110 minutes - capable of two showings per night rather than one - Trumbo's script was sliced and diced, and *The Horsemen* never charged out of the gate at the box office when it reached the theaters in late 1971.

Singing sensation Barbra Streisand became a movie star with the release of *Funny Girl* in 1968, and producer Ray Stark was looking to build on her success. Stark hired playwright Arthur Laurents to create a vehicle for her which resulted in the screenplay for *The Way We Were* about an unlikely romance between Streisand's politically motivated campus radical and Robert Redford's upper class writer with dreams of being a novelist but also willing to sell out for Hollywood paychecks. When Pollack was not satisfied with Laurents' final draft he was dismissed, and 11 other writers were brought in to bring magic to the script.

Dalton Trumbo could certainly bring life experience to both characters. He wrote 16 pages that included scenes involving the HUAC hearings. Although both Redford and Streisand were partial towards Trumbo's politicized take on the story, Stark and Pollock ultimately decided to lean more heavily on the love story and brought back Laurents - at a much steeper rate. The re-tooled *The Way We Were*, set in the era of the Red Scare, went on to become one of the most popular romantic dramas in Hollywood history without Trumbo's 16 pages.

Edward Lewis had been a producer on *Spartacus* and four other movies made of Dalton Trumbo's words and David Miller had directed *Lonely Are The Brave* from Trumbo's "perfect script", so when the duo wanted to make a movie of the John F. Kennedy assassination from a story by Donald Freed and Mark Lane but found the script impossible to film, it was natural they would turn to Trumbo. Lewis wanted a movie that would depict a conspiracy in the killing of the President. Trumbo was never rooted in the conspiracy camp but after looking over the Warren Commission report on the assassination and watching an uncut version of the home movie of the shooting taken by Abraham Zapruder, he became convinced that Kennedy had been struck by bullets fired from two directions. Working backwards from that premise, Trumbo concocted his conspiracy plot for *Executive Action*.

While Miller and Trumbo never assert that anything in the film is actually true, neither do they dissuade viewers that the events might have occurred. The movie ends with a photo collage of 18 material witnesses to the Kennedy assassination who were identified after November 22, 1963, and 16 were dead of unnatural causes within three years. A British mathematician estimates that the odds against all these people dying in so short a time is 100,000 trillion to one and viewers are left to draw their own conclusions. Released in 1973, Executive Action was the first of many Hollywood films to posit a hidden conspiracy in Kennedy's death.

In the early 1970s, the true life account of Henri Charrière's escape from France's notorious penal colonies in French Guinea and Devil's Island prison became one of Hollywood's hottest properties. Superstar Steve McQueen was set to play the role of Charriere, known as "Papillon" - the Butterfly - from a tattoo on his chest. McQueen was reported to be the first actor to ever receive two million dollars up front for a movie when he signed on to *Papillon* to be directed by Franklin J. Schaffner.

William Goldman wrote the first draft of the screenplay that was faithful to Henri Charrière's book but when it was decided to expand one of the characters to be the equal of Papillon the screenwriter was committed to another picture. In February 1973, Dustin Hoffman was cast to play opposite McQueen and Dalton Trumbo hired to bulk up his character of Louis Dega, who had been a minor player in the book.

Hoffman and Trumbo spent long hours in discussions and as the actor came to know the screenwriter he became charmed by the veteran Hollywood wordsmith's personal cocktail of sophistication, toughness and integrity. Hoffman suggested that Trumbo write Dega's character as himself while he trundled off to the New York Public Library to check out everything he could find on French penal colonies. When Goldman saw the completed movie with Dega-as-Trumbo he remarked that only one line he wrote remained on the screen.

Since Schaffner and his crew were working with a fluid, unfinished script, Trumbo was required to be on location for the shoot in Spain and in Jamaica where an elaborate prison set was constructed. Trumbo did more than invest the film with his feisty personality for the character of Louis Dega. When the actor who was all set to play the prison commandant who dispatched the prisoners to Devil's Island was barred from the set by the Screen Actors Guild, there was no time to find a replacement and Trumbo was recruited for the part.

In his nearly four decades in Hollywood, Dalton Trumbo had done a lot of things: he had invented stories, adapted screenplays, directed a movie and even contributed a voice over or two. But he had never appeared in a movie. He was not eager to appear in this one, either, especially since he would have to have his hair cut. But appear he did, and as the cameras rolled Trumbo delivered his only lines on the silver screen:

"As for France, the nation has disposed of you. France has rid herself of you altogether. Forget France. And put your clothes on."

Papillon premiered in Los Angeles on December 18, 1973. Today, the movie is considered a classic but it received mixed reviews around its holiday opening, although McQueen was singled out for doing the best work of his career. The premiere was a benefit for the Western Institute for Cancer and Leukemia Research as a tribute to Henri Charrière, who had died of lung cancer five months before shooting began.

There would be several other benefit premieres in the coming months but there would be another honoree besides Henri Charrière; during the production of *Papillon* Dalton Trumbo was also diagnosed with lung cancer.

Chapter 6: Death and Legacy

Trumbo had smoked six packs of cigarettes a day for most of his adult life. Increasingly he began suffering bouts of illness that were affecting his work. When revisions were needed to the script of *Executive Action* at the last minute, he was too ill to make the adjustments and another member of the Hollywood Ten, Alvah Bessie, was called on to do the re-write. After he became sick on *Papillon*, his son Christopher was called in to polish up the script.

Today, lung cancer causes more deaths than the next three most toxic cancers - colon, breast and pancreatic - combined. The five-year survival rate is 16 percent compared with 64 percent for colon cancer, 89 percent for breast cancer and 99 percent for prostate cancer. In 1973, a diagnosis of lung cancer was much worse. The first successful lung transplants were still a decade away and the link with smoking, first suspected in the 1930s, had not been fully accepted until the 1960s. The ban on advertising of cigarettes on television and radio had only just begun in 1971.

Trumbo's diagnosis was not unexpected. Career retrospectives were already being assembled. His collected correspondence of letters written to family and others was rounded up and published in the well-reviewed book, Additional Dialogue, in 1970. That same year, the Writers Guild of America honored Trumbo with The Laurel Award for Screenwriting Achievement in advancing the literature of the motion picture through the years. The only other member of the Hollywood Ten who would be so feted would be Ring Lardner, Jr. in 1989.

To try and stem the cancer, Trumbo had a lung removed in 1973. Certainly his mother would not have been surprised by her son's diagnosis of a death sentence later in life. After her husband died, Maud Trumbo railed against her son's heavy smoking and drinking in the house. The serious rows between the two extended into politics where the mother of the convicted Communist was a staunch Republican her entire life.

In spite of their differences, Trumbo never lost affection for his mother. After he buried her at the end of her 82 years in 1967, he recalled that anything he ever did that might be considered rebellious stemmed from his mother. He pointed out that, when she was a young woman, she did something braver and more radical in its way than anything he ever attempted when Maud walked away from her church and took up with Christian Scientists in her devout community.

Even Steve Martin's passing acquaintance with Trumbo through his daughter yielded obvious signs of a troublesome future due to the screenwriter's life choices. Martin recalled that Trumbo tried to cut back on his drinking by smoking pot instead, and his daily exercise routine consisted of walking laps around his swimming pool while inhaling cigarettes.

On May 17, 1975, Dalton Trumbo finally received the Oscar for his screenplay of The Brave One that had gone unclaimed 19 years earlier. Walter Mirisch, who had been the producer of Hawaii, brought the 18-pound statuette to Trumbo's Beverly Hills home. He would live just 15 months more before succumbing to congestive heart failure on September 10, 1976.

Dalton Trumbo continued to write throughout his final act, leaving behind a jumble of never-produced screenplays, half-fleshed out projects and unpublished prose. A partly-written novel about World War II seen through the eyes of a concentration camp commandant that Trumbo had gnawed on for 16 years was completed by Robert Kirsch and published by Viking Press in 1979 as *Night of the Aurochs*. The only posthumous film project to come to fruition would be *Ishi: The Last of His Tribe*, about an Indian who turned up on a Northern California ranch in 1911 from a tribe so small no one living in the area had ever heard of it. The screenplay is an adaptation of the book by a San Francisco anthropologist who befriended the last surviving member of the Yahi.

Christopher Trumbo finished up the screenplay from his father's beginnings and sold the movie to NBC Television which aired the biopic in 1978. Otto Preminger had given the younger Trumbo a job as assistant director on *Exodus* when he was just out of high school. After graduating from Columbia University in New York City Christopher began working as a screenwriter in television and the movies in 1967 at the age of 26.

After Ishi: The Last of His Tribe Christopher Trumbo sold a few more episodic television scripts but notoriety would not return until the early 2000s when he sculpted a play out of his father's letters written while on the Hollywood blacklist. *Trumbo: Red, White and Blacklisted* opened off-Broadway in the 1890s Romanesque Revival-styled Westside Theatre in New York City and ran for one year. Tony Award-winning actor Nathan Lane opened the production playing Dalton Trumbo and was followed in the role by such transcendent talents as Chris Cooper, Richard Dreyfuss, Gore Vidal and F. Murray Abraham. Brian Dennehy, who won a Tony Award in "Death of a Salesman," took the show on a national tour as Trumbo.

Trumbo turned his play into a movie documentary that was released in 2007. Dennehy and Lane returned for the film version and were joined by Liam Neeson, Paul Giamatti, David Strathairn, Joan Allen, Donald Sutherland and Michael Douglas. The movie featured an interview with Kirk Douglas, then in his 90s, who had helped crack the blacklist by publicly hiring Dalton Trumbo a half century earlier. Christopher Trumbo became a go-to expert to comment on the Hollywood blacklist and was working on a book on the era when he died in 1911. Christopher Trumbo was 70 years old when he passed away - the same age as his father.

Cleo Fincher Trumbo lived nearly as long her son. She died in 2009 at the age of 93. In 1993 she appeared before an audience at the Academy Theater in Los Angeles to accept the Oscar for her husband's story for *Roman Holiday*. Forty years overdue, Dalton Trumbo had now received both Oscars he had won while blacklisted by Hollywood.

The Trumbos' oldest child, Nikola, grew up to lead a private life as a psychotherapist. The youngest, Mitzi, channeled her artistic impulses into photography. Once, while prowling her house looking for subjects, she happened upon her father in his favorite writing spot - soaking in a tub, cigarette holder in hand with his typewriter resting on a board laid across the porcelain bath. He was scrawling on an easel when he looked up to see his daughter, camera in hand. That photograph became ubiquitous and appears to this day anytime something is written about Trumbo.

Trumbo preferred to write in his tub late at night. Cleo would recall times when he would spend days soaking and writing and smoking. Kirk Douglas told of the time he gave Trumbo a parrot as a gift and the parrot would sit on the writer's shoulder "pecking Dalton's ear while Dalton pecked at the keys."

Dalton Trumbo's professional papers were so extensive that they are located in three different university archives. He saw his own legacy being the novel he wrote when he was 33 years old, *Johnny Got His Gun*. The book went through 40 printings and was eulogized by the Los Angeles Times as "perhaps the most effective anti-war novel ever written in America." Trumbo himself once said just a few years before his death, "The novel is obviously the best thing I've ever done. Maybe the one good thing I've done."

At the University of Colorado, where Trumbo spent a year of his aborted college career, a "free speech" fountain was erected outside the University Memorial Center and named after him. But the most appropriate memorial to the blacklisted screenwriter is 250 miles west, where Dalton Trumbo first put pen to paper and got paid for it.

In 2004, on the eve of the anniversary of Dalton Trumbo's 100th birthday, Christopher Trumbo traveled to Grand Junction to present his play and speak about his father, the fond stories he told his kids about growing up in Colorado, and about his role breaking the Hollywood blacklist. His appearance spawned renewed interest in the town's most famous native son.

A committee of teachers and historians formed to plan activities to honor Trumbo during his centennial year. Over the muted objections of a few dissenters who remembered their parents' ruffled feathers, it was decided to reprint *Eclipse* and the Trumbo family happily gave the novel's copyright to the local library. Nikola Trumbo wrote an introduction assuring townsfolk of her father's love for the town. The library ended up selling almost 2,000 copies.

Grand Junction staged a film festival of Trumbo movies and held a 100th birthday dinner. There were even tours of local Eclipse landmarks and sights. Most importantly, the new Trumbophiles announced plans to create a statue of Dalton Trumbo based on Mitzi Trumbo's photograph of her father in his bathtub.

When the Grand Junction City Council decided that a statue of a naked 62-year old man in a bathtub was not the best way to spend voter's money, the local citizenry raised $44,000 for the bronze casting on its own. The sculpture by artist J. Michael Wilson was dedicated on October 13, 2007. Trumbo sits in the antique bathtub with coffee at the ready and cigarette in hand while he works on a script. A bronze rubber duckie floats on the water. Dalton Trumbo is home at last.

Bibliography

American Lung Cancer Association, Lung Cancer Fact Sheet.

American Masters, Public Broadcasting System, August 11, 2009.

American National Biography Online, Trumbo, Dalton (1905 - 1976), Screenwriters, Fiction Writers, February 2000.

Black, Louis, The Austin Chronicle, "Page Two: The Time of the Toad," November 3, 2006.

Bogle, Chalres, World Socialist Web Site, "Hollywood on Trial: a timely reminder," December 10, 2009.

Capshaw, Ron, An Interdisciplinary Journal of North American Studies, "Americanism with a Vengeance: Civil Liberties and Dalton Trumbo," June 20, 2002.

Cieply, Michael, The New York Times, "A Voice From the Blacklist: Documentary Lets Dalton Trumbo Speak (Through Surrogates)," September 11, 2007.

Douglas, Kirk, The Ragman's Son, New York: Pocket Books, 1988.

Ebert, Chicago Sun Times, "Johnny Got His Gun," January 1, 1971.

Ebert, Chicago Sun Times, "Remembering Dalton Trumbo," September 14, 1976.

Encyclopedia of World Biography, Dalton Trumbo, 2004.

Feeney, F.X, Written By, "Odd Man: In The Legacy of Dalton Trumbo," February 2002.

Georgakas, Dan, Encyclopedia of the American Left, "The Hollywood Blacklist," 1992.

Gulliford, Andrew, The Durango Herald, "Writer on the fringe," January 7, 2011.

Hanson, Peter, Dalton Trumbo, Hollywood Rebel: A Critical Survey and Filmography, North Carolina: McFarland & Company, 2000.

LaSalle, Mick, San Francisco Chronicle, "He was blacklisted in a national witch hunt. Yet writer Dalton Trumbo never lost his integrity," March 3, 2005.

Martin, Steve, Born Standing Up: A Comic's Life, New York: Scribner, 2007.

Marx, Andy, Variety, "Acad honors Trumbo for 'Roman Holiday'," May 12, 1993.

McLellan, Dennis, Los Angeles Times, "Cleo Trumbo dies at 93; wife of blacklisted screenwriter Dalton Trumbo," October 18, 2009.

McLellan, Dennis, Los Angeles Times, "Christopher Trumbo dies at 70; screen and TV writer whose father was blacklisted," January 12, 2011.

New York Daily News, "Dalton Trumbo went from A-list to blacklist," June 21, 2008.

Nichols, Josh, Grand Junction Free Press, "Moyer's turn: After honoring Walker, Grand Junction group looks to next Legend," February 10, 2009.

Nijhuis, Michelle, San Francisco Chronicle, "The hometown that forgave Dalton Trumbo," March 5, 2006.

Nordheimer, Jon, The New York Times; "Trumbo, Blacklisted for 10 Years By the Film Industry, Dies at 70," September 11, 1976.

Palmer, Tim, Cinema Journal, "Side of the Angels: Dalton Trumbo, the Hollywood Trade Press, and the Blacklist," Summer, 2005.

Radosh, Ronald, National Review, "Will the New Trumbo Movie Rehash Old Myths," November 2, 2013.

Schreiber, Rebecca Mina, Cold War Exiles in Mexico: U.S. Dissidents and the Culture of Critical Resistance, Minneapolis: University of Minnesota Press, 2008.

Smith, Kyle, Commentary, "The Friends of Dalton Trumbo," January 1, 2007.

The Fredericksburg Free-Lance Star; "Dustin Hoffman Absorbs Role of Louis Dega," April 4, 1974.

The Hollywood Reporter; "Bryan Cranston to Star as Blacklisted Screenwriter Dalton Trumbo," Septmeber 18, 2013.

Trex, Ethan, Mental Floss, "Who Is Dalton Trumbo? 5 Facts About Bryan Cranston's Next Role," September 19, 2013.

Trumbo, Dalton, Additional dialogue; letters of Dalton Trumbo, 1942-1962, New York: M. Evans, 1970.

Van Gelder, Lawrence, The New York Times;
"Lionel Stander Dies at 86; Actor Who Defied
Blacklist," December 2, 1994.

Wisconsin Center for Film & Theater Research,
The Hollywood Blacklist Collections, "Dalton
Trumbo," 2007.

18363354R00059

Printed in Poland
by Amazon Fulfillment
Poland Sp. z o.o., Wrocław